Touching Nature

Musings on Life and Living

Kamal Advani

2017

Contents

Copyright	i
Dedication	iii
Foreword by Kang Endar	v
Preface	vii

I.	**Essentials**	**1**
1.	Fire	3
2.	Water	7
3.	Air	11
4.	Earth	15
II.	**Scapes**	**19**
5.	The Beach: A Confluence	21
6.	Night Sky	25

Contents

7. Mount Wombat   29

8. Shade of the Oak   33

9. Lotus in the Temple Pond   39

Afterword   43

About the Author   45

Colophon   47

Copyright

Touching Nature: *Musings on Life and Living*
© 2017 Kamal Advani

All rights reserved. This material may not be reproduced, displayed, modified, or distributed without the express prior written permission of the copyright holder.

Dedication

MST/AJ
My Parents and Ancestors
My Teachers, Masters, and Guides
My Almamater, the BKC

*Nature does not hurry,
yet everything is accomplished.*

—Lao Tzu

Foreword by Kang Endar[1]

As my student who invariably listens to his master's advice on *life and living*, Kamal understands the balanced harmony between him and his surrounds. His distinctive approach to searching for meaning in Nature around us is special in that it seeks to *awaken* one's awareness of one's intricate link to Nature.

If you seek life's pearls and wisdom, and you wish to be able to better see and feel the spirit's oneness with Nature, then this book is an excellent choice.

May your read be both enjoyable, and beneficial.

—

Endar
5th *Dan*, BKC
Head Instructor, Depok Branch — West Java, Indonesia

---

1   *Kang* is a Sundanese — a dialect of West Java, Indonesia — term meaning 'brother'. *Kang* Endar is the author's main *Karaté* master. This foreword was provided in Bahasa Indonesia, *Kang* Endar's native tongue, it is thus translated — hopefully accurately!

Preface

Spending time in Nature — simply contemplating, or practicing *Karaté* — one cannot help but be in awe of creation. Submerged in the moment — only to emerge with a fresher, clearer outlook on life.

It is these small epiphanies, these many small *satori*[1], that the author wishes to put into words.

Language and literary tools have limitations when it comes to something so experiential. However, intent and impressions transcend words. Do join the author on this mutual journey, even if separated by spacetime.

Applied, Validated Wisdom

The author has strived to apply the wisdom gained, making sure the writing is not without substance. However, there are cases where the author intuitively knows something to be true, but due to the stage of life he is in, has no direct experience of it. Weighing that it may still be beneficial to others in that stage, the author has written the thoughts that come through.

---
1 Enlightenment: https://en.wikipedia.org/wiki/Satori

Preface

Format

For each theme explored, there is a musing/poetry, accompanied by a commentary expanding on the musing. The musings, to an extent, take inspiration from *Zen Kōan*[2], favouring simplicity and compactness over aesthetic and adherence to literary rules.

Life and Living

The phrase "Life and Living" is from the Karate school the author trains at, the *Bandung Karate Club* (BKC) — where one of the core tenets is to strive to *learn the meaning of life and living*.

'Living' is a broad term, but in essence it covers our interactions with our surroundings, Nature, and fellow living beings. The book seeks to show that much can be learned about life and living by contemplating Nature.

Relationships deepen with investment — by understanding one another over a period of time. The relationship one has with Nature is no different. The reader is encouraged to go out into Nature to experience the book's musings.

---

2 Parables, questions, or, phrases intended to invoke a psychospiritual reaction in a practitioner's mind, to force them to reflect deeper, e.g., 'What is the sound of one hand clapping?', see https://en.wikipedia.org/wiki/K%C5%8Dan

Motivation

This book is as much for the author as it is for an audience. The author continues to study and apply the teachings he is provided with, and as is human, sometimes fails to apply them.

The same lessons become clearer with time and in new contexts. Most recently, the author had an experience with a tenet he has known for over twenty four years. While he had some inkling that there was a quality most profound, and most 'literal' about that tenet, he simply read it as an interesting philosophical life guideline. But after an intensive training session with a senior teacher of his one late evening, it was as if a set of pearls came elegantly strung together.

The necklace formed was that one tenet.

This book is no doctrine; merely the creative output of a seeker, who feels he has reached a point where his understanding is, perhaps, *stable* enough to share. The author's hope is that what is shared here is universal to the human condition.

Acknowledgements

First and foremost, the author acknowledges his parents, for their love, and for always providing for him. And more contemporarily, for not (visibly) panicking that their son has decided to take an extended leave with no concrete plan[3]. To his sister, who provided interesting and healthy meals while he wrote.

---

3   Relax, I have guidelines!

Preface

Kang Endar, who has taught him more about living than any education ever could. *Kang* Ray, who treats each student like a diamond in the rough. *Kang* Trisula, senior teacher and friend, who constantly encourages his endeavours, and heart-melded with him on the Lotus, the subject of **Chapter 9**.

Our Grandmaster and Guide, *Kang* Iwa Rahadian Arsanata, for providing us with the BKC — a school that forges us into better humans, and so much more.

Ade Ishs[4], closest of friends, artist extraordinaire, provided plenty of input on typography and aesthetics. Brendan Griffiths, friend and student, provided critical input on writing style and layout aesthetics. *Senpai* Gerrard Warburton, senior and friend, kindly acted as a tour guide through **Mt. Wombat**.

---

4   If you like cool, contemporary jazz, Ade's your man: http://www.adeishs.com/

Essentials

1. Fire

The Embers.
Faint they may become
Yet always there.

A gateway are the Embers.
Stoke, and coax them
Gently, but resolutely.

At times, by pure desire.
At others, by lack thereof.
A gateway are the Embers
To the Fire of the Soul.

When found
Be consumed only
By the Pure Fire.

Of its Raging Twin
Beware.

1. Fire

Commentary

Fire reflects desire. In many cultures and teachings, though perhaps most prominently, in the Yoga idea of *Chakras*[1], the fire element is the symbol of the navel chakra. The seat of desire. Easy to see when one considers the lure of food and how it relates to the stomach!

An ambition that is too *fiery* ends up burning even what is seeked after. The lack of happiness one finds at the end of a journey, having burnt everything along the way to get there, is typical in current society.

On the other hand, a lack of drive is also commonplace. People who have no desire to achieve anything, either physical, or spiritual floating about aimlessly through.

In this universe of duals, desire must be counterbalanced by curbing excessive desires. To focus on desires that matter. Such self-control begets a will of Fire.

Fulfilment of Desires: Physical and Spiritual

The one management theory that has stuck with the author is Maslow's Hierachy of Needs. See Fig. 1.1.

The pyramid agrees with ancient ideas of fulfilment — that one must satisfy body, mind, and spirit.

---

[1] Simplifying: there are 7 major energy vortices, called *chakras* — 'wheel' in sanskrit — on the spirit body, and many smaller ones which act as a gateway to taking in and releasing energy, like pores on the skin, regulating many psychospiritual and physical functions of the body. See http://healing.about.com/cs/chakras/a/learnchakras.htm, for example.

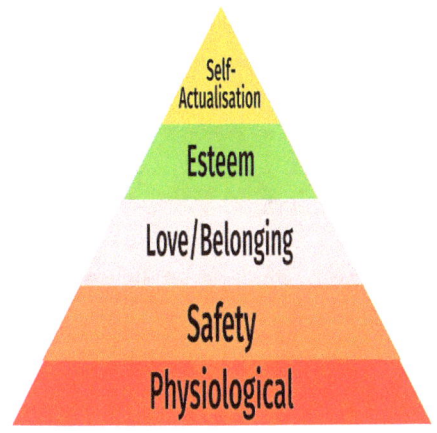

Figure 1.1.: Maslow's Hierarchy of Needs

When one's stomach is hungry, one can't think beyond this primal need to survive, but slowly as base desires for survival are satisfied, inevitably we seek more. Unfortunately, this need is translated, by some, to seek more physical fulfilments rather than going deeper into oneself!

While the representation shows a hierarchy, spiritual progress is made *in parallel* to worldly progress, and in the most difficult of situations — indeed, major progress is made in difficult situations.

Arguably, the world is a vehicle for spiritual progress, for otherwise, one has no gauge to measure spiritual progress against. Can one claim to have learned patience if one is constantly blowing up at circumstances?

Except, perhaps, in cases where one's worldly endeavours are actively destructive to society — and perhaps it is then time to change

1. Fire

jobs! — there is no major conflict in seeking both spiritual and physical fulfilment. One finds that seeking the spiritual tends to affect one's worldly behaviour anyhow.

Breaking Patterns of Desires

Practices such as fasting, or more generally, applying constraints for a fixed amount of time, have many physical and spiritual benefits. It is the most straightforward approach of measuring willpower, of curbing desires.

If one is a big foodie, constraining food will be the challenge. If one is a big movie person, reduce going to the movies or watching television for a fixed period.

This is the core idea behind such *spiritual tools* — to provide an *alternative* view or feeling, to break a pattern, by, for a pre-determined period of time, stopping what one does almost automatically.

Finally, while the author focuses on desires, such practices have benefits far beyond just curbing desires. At the very least, one starts to think about how else to apply the time now available.

2. Water

What can be said of Water
That has not already been said.

Age after Age
As Water flows
So do its Aphorisms
Flow down the Stream of Time.

In one Moment
A gentle stream
Adapt and Move
Bend and Flow
Seduce the mild obstacles.

In Another
A Mighty Wave
Permeate and Fathom
Persist and Crash
Break through the Unyielding.

2. Water

Commentary

A lot has been said about Water's adaptability. How it becomes what contains it. Adaptability, the ability to accommodate circumstances are indeed precious skills of a peaceful life, to 'go with the flow'.

Plenty of things take time to change, and it is better to work around limitations much of the time, than fight the system. To be reasonable, as it were.

However, not much is said about the negative states of Water.

The wisdom of Water is achieved in knowing not only if it can change forms, but also when to change forms, and what form to take.

Stagnant Water

Water flows because of external factors. The wind and the moon's gravity affect the waves. If left alone, Water stays still as if without any further dynamic. In a state of stagnation, one is constantly being led rather than leading.

In the author's view, and perhaps, due to rather strong biases from life experiences, the wisdom of being unreasonable is underrated. It leads to problems that stick around due to the sheer inertia of solving them, rather than some truly fundamental basis. Doing something inefficiently, never improving on it, because "that's the way it's always been done" reeks of stagnant Water.

Consider also that stagnant water often implies gunk and heavier objects in the water, taking away from the flowing nature of water.

Commentary

Flowing

A balance is achieved when one knows when to flow, and when one must *change the direction of flow*. Life has many tributaries. Flowing through particular ones is a choice that must sometimes be made.

Stillness and Taking the Lower Position

The author can say it no better here than Chapter 61 of the *Tao Te Ching*. Using Hamill's translation[1]:

*A great state should flow down
like a river, the world's confluence.*

*The world is feminine,
feminine in constant stillness
overcoming the masculine.*

To be still, take the lower position.

*Therefore the great state
lowers itself for the smaller.*

*Small states that are lower
are governed by the great state.*

Small states lower themselves

---

[1] The author's copy is Sam Hamill's *Tao Te Ching: A New Translation*, see http://amzn.to/2moRtJF. On the web, several translation comparisons are found at http://www.egreenway.com/taoism/ttclz61.htm

2. Water

to achieve accord with a great one.

*Thus some lower themselves to govern,
others lower themselves to be governed.*

*A great state mostly wants unity, nurturing people.
A small state wants most to enter the service of
the people.*

*For both to fulfill their wishes,
the greater must become lower.*

The verse uses behaviour of states or nations as an example, though it equally applies to human behaviour. The essence of it is a *winning by losing* attitude. To flow downward, to humble oneself, is not losing in the grand scheme of things.

There are times, where even if one is right, it is simply better to be diplomatic, apologise, and move on. This is particularly true in heated situations with loved ones. The grand scheme is to maintain a loving relationship. One moment of being humble and accepting is a small price to pay.

On the idea of stillness, an illustrative comparison is *stillness in motion* — a core idea in Martial Arts. Seemingly contradictory when put into words, it simply emphasises a calm mind directing a moving body.

At a micro level, we may be performing a movement, or sparring with a partner. At a macro level, it is to maintain an inner calm in a chaotic situation.

3. Air

Medium of Quintessence.

Forego Food and Water
One may.
But Air?

Freedom manifested.
Flight Lord.

When sad
When shackled
When in disarray
When in doubt

Breathe...

Commentary

Paraphrasing my Grandmaster, we often hear of people fasting, foregoing food and water for days, both for spiritual reasons, and those involuntarily surviving ordeals. We also have accounts speak

3. Air

of saints, and today, magicians undergoing air deprivation. But never beyond a few hours, if that.

Physically, and metaphysically, air carries the essences of life.

Consider that when one is afraid, when one is tied down by the problems of life, one breathes more shallowly. Sicknesses attack more easily.

The phrase oft used is to "go get some air". A wise choice.

On Freedom vs. Action

Air characterises freedom of the highest order. To move about at will, unstoppable. Yet, the application of constraints to excessive freedom is what produces wonders.

Given infinite time, and infinite resources, it is likely that nothing will come out of it.

To be more meaningful, Air must guide and direct elements such as Fire, Water, and Earth towards producing something of value. Consider how air carries nutrients, either directly or indirectly by guiding the other elements across nature.

Living in Australia, the author has become aware of the role of bush fires, driven by wind, as being vital in maintaining entire ecosystems of flora and fauna[1].

One must balance total freedom with the desire and willingness to work with others towards something greater.

---

1 https://en.wikipedia.org/wiki/Fire_ecology

Air, then, also represents power, a gateway towards directing the other elements of life.

On Wandering vs. Action

One cannot help but consider the idea of wandering when thinking of Air. A favourite quote of the author is by J.R.R. Tolkien in *The Fellowship of the Ring*[2]:

> Not all those who wander are lost

There is no such thing as wandering aimlessly, it is just that the aim is not yet known.

The wisdom of Air is in knowing when to wander, and when to act. When in wandering, one sees no bigger picture yet, one can but act on the smaller picture.

In acting, in taking steps, the aim of the wandering is discovered.[3]

Finally, if wandering for an extended period, be sure to have supplies for the road ahead.

---

[2] The author has not read the book, sorry! Credits: https://www.goodreads.com/quotes/299192-not-all-those-who-wander-are-lost

[3] A software analogy — though sometimes taken too far — might be the idea of *emergent design*.

4. Earth

Ancient is the Mother
Ever nurturing
Ever protective.

Good and Evil
Beautiful and Grotesque
All She accommodates.

All She accepts
At the end of their Times.

Always transforming Death
Into Rebirth.

Touch Her
And be Linked
With all Beings.

Commentary

The Earth is non-discrimination and bountifulness manifested. She both gives and takes. Considering her transformative ability: the

4. Earth

ability to take nutrients, to decompose things into their parts, and then only to grow new life-supporting beings... even her taking is a form of giving. In perhaps a better sense, more often than not, she *accepts* rather than takes.

From the perspective of an element, Earth signifies steadfastness and stability. It also signifies connectedness: a *common ground* for all beings.

In prior chapters on the elements, the author was able to isolate discussion more or less purely to the element itself. Here, it feels more appropriate to discuss both the element, and our planet as a whole.

The Earthesque Nature of Principles vs. Application

Principles held by one need to be as solid as Earth. However, applying those principles requires collaboration with the other elements. Excessive rigidity rarely yields success.

While Earth represents the unmoving, the other elements are much more dynamic. Good principles — *solid principles* — remain the same across Time. That is, after all, the sign of good principle: to be true regardless of context.

However, everyone lives within a context. As such, principles, their interpretation, and most certainly their application must apply within that context. Context is very much *unlike* Earth. It constantly changes with time. Each Age comes with differing cultures, mindsets, and technological advancements.

As Water, the application of principles must be adapted to the times.

It is for this reason, in the author's view, that religious teachings seem quaint, out of place, and out of context in the contemporary world. Religious principles remain as true as ever. However, the associated dogma that has been solidified with the *core*[1] teachings is what is out of place.

The original elucidations of the core teachings, meant to be fluid, and to be applied in a particular cultural setting, have been carried forward, and given the same Earth-like qualities as the core.

Contemporary guides are criticised by the uninspired — and by those who use religion as a tool only to control others — for modernising the elucidations. For not conforming to a section of a teaching that does not actually seek conformity. It seeks an application appropriate for its time[2].

The author never ceases to be amazed, amused, and dejected — all at the same time — by the irony of calling God great, but then limiting this greatness to a shallow, uninspired interpretation of a few pages of a book.

The Strength of Humility

Consider phrases such as 'being down to earth', and 'staying grounded' — imploring one to be humble rather than proud and lofty. The Earth is quite literally stepped upon every single day. Were the Earth not resilient, we would not survive.

---

1 Is it not interesting that we associated words like 'core' with the Earth?
2 For the Unix geeks, a workable analogy is the Rule of Separation, http://www.catb.org/~esr/writings/taoup/html/ch01s06.html#id2877777, or for the functional programmers, a pure function applied to a changing environment.

4. Earth

The low has just as much to offer as the high[3].

It is often noted that the higher one goes, the worse the fall. Unless, of course, one is grounded, rooted to the Earth.

---

[3] A point that some corporate types fail — rather miserably — to understand.

Scapes

5. The Beach: A Confluence

Wind guiding the Waves.
Water and Earth
Meet as Old Friends.

What of Fire?

Rekindle
Fire of the Soul.

Be merged
In the Confluence.

Commentary

Looking far into the vast oceans, Air in the skies raises one's spirits high, while at the same time the Water brings deep respite to one's soul. All the while, the sands keeps one grounded.

The beach is an interesting confluence of the elements. It dawned upon the author that one comes back from the beach recharged, invigorated, electrified. Electricity being a manifestation of primarily Fire.

5. The Beach: A Confluence

At a beach, or a forest with a river, then, humans and living beings bring the Fire element. These confluences allow us to explore our connectedness to Nature much more deeply.

Microcosmos and Macrocosmos

The human being — body and spirit — is another such confluence.

The ancient idea of the human as being a microcosmos, a hologram of the macrocosmos/Universe are interestingly both metaphorical, as expected, but perhaps somewhat unexpectedly, quite literal.

Physically, flesh and bones are earthesque, providing us with structural integrity. However, 50-60% of the body is Water manifesting in the various fluids. We breathe in Air, of course. As stated previously, our spirit is as Fire.

The ratio of Water to Earth is interesting, in a sense, we are meant to be more fluid and flexible than stiff or overly constrained in the way we act.

Some seek to control Nature. Phrases such as 'conquering Nature' are often used by immature industrialists and adventurers. It would follow, rather logically then, that in conquering Nature, one would be conquering oneself. If we used the word 'conquer' in a destructive sense here, destroying our surrounds is destroying ourself.

All very obvious, yet the state of the world does not reflect said obviousness.

Taking this obviousness further, taking care of Nature is hardly a selfless act!

Knowing Oneself through Nature

Appreciating the wisdom and beauty of nature causes one to almost automatically reflect within — as experienced by many who find it easier to relax and meditate in natural settings.

Lao Tzu of *Tao Te Ching* fame[1], said:

> "Knowing others is wisdom, knowing yourself is Enlightenment."

While the author does not know if there is one grand enlightenment to be achieved, there are certainly many small and large enlightenments that we obtain as we go through life. Nature's confluences are great allies in finding ourselves when we most need to.

---

1   Unable to find the exact text this came from, plenty of references without sources on the Internet, e.g., https://www.brainyquote.com/quotes/quotes/l/laotzu110063.html

6. Night Sky

Sublime Darkness.

Starscape Supreme
Moonscape Divine.

Pacifier of the turbulent heart
Evoking Stillness of Being.

Charmer of the Night Creatures
Visible and Invisible
Of this Dimension and Beyond.

Gazing at the Night Stars
The Gazees gaze back.

At the Grandeur of the Night Sky
Fathom.

In its Quietude
Respite.

6. Night Sky

Commentary

The night is a magical time where different human faculties become more awake. Faculties of reflection and contemplation. The quietude allowing us to connect more directly with the subtle frequencies of Nature. Our environment comes to a standstill, the worries of the day dissolved, if for a few hours. A clarity of a different kind, like a light shone on a dark corner of a room, arises.

Nocturnal creatures come out to play, a whole new world awakes. It is no coincidence that many creatives work in the early hours of the morning, or late at night, where the nocturnal energy is still palpable. (And yes, it is quieter, too!).

Light vs. Dark: The World of Dualities

The character Melisandre[1] said in *Game of Thrones*, that the "night is dark and full of terrors". This musing prefers not to dwell on Lady Melisandre's view. An awesome quote, nevertheless.

Slightly more seriously, Dark and Light are part of the world's dualities. Illustrated beautifully and brilliantly by the Yin-Yang symbol (Fig. 6.1).

The symbol shows the interdependence of dark and light, or more generally, the opposing forces of the universe. Note that each major force enters into each other's spaces. The circle is not a cleanly divided half.

---

1   http://gameofthrones.wikia.com/wiki/Melisandre

Figure 6.1.: Taijitu: Yin-Yang Symbol

Furthermore, even within light there is some darkness, and within darkness there is some light, shown by the small circles of opposing colours in the major halves.

One cannot exist without the other. That is to say, the human mind cannot see one without having the contrast of the opposite.

Though, eventually we must see the wisdom of both and where appropriate, transcend the duality. *Transcending is not apathy*, it is to understand more clearly that not all is what it seems.

The duality of the world is clear in phrases such as 'a lesser evil', 'deals with the devil', 'a white lie', and 'playing good cop, bad cop'.

We realise that things will never be entirely perfect, for by the same token, *perfection cannot exist without imperfection*. We see the wisdom in applying either power, in balance, to achieve our goals.

6. *Night Sky*

Relatives vs. Absolutes

Contemplating duality, one wonders if relatives are all there are in the world.

It only takes a little bit of further contemplation — to consider the *absolute* and *unconditional* love that exists between people, lovers, parent and child — to know that innate and absolute beauty, light, and goodness do exist.

Unfortunately, as does absolute wrong. The dual forces, after all, are contained absolutely in one big circle.

While anchoring ourselves to the absolute good, we navigate the shades of grey.

7. Mount Wombat

Tranquil Terrain
Of Rocks and Woodlands.

A Mild Hike
Of Contemplative Awareness.

In Peacefulness and Freedom
One is immersed.
Impeled, if not by Choice.

Behold the smoothened Rocks
Ancient and Mighty
As Gentle Giants
Welcoming those Worthy.

In the Here and Now
Acknowledge
Past Impressions
Of the Aboriginal Folk.

7. Mount Wombat

Commentary

The Mt. Wombat Reserve[1] is a National Park in Victoria, Australia about 180 km (112 miles) from the Melbourne CBD.

There are many, many more aesthetically pleasing areas in Australia, of course. However, places are defined not only by their aesthetics, but also the impressions, the *feeling* they carry.

Applying this perspective, there is a certain ancient calmness that defines Mt. Wombat. The author visited Mt. Wombat during the summer season, where it isn't nearly as beautiful as it is in Spring, at least physically. Yet this lack of physical aesthetics makes it easier to see other dimensions.

In particular, the rock formations, as if like communities and families of their own, is awe inspiring.

Bloodlines

An anecdote that the author cannot confirm by way of written record (at least, not in the limited research done by the author), is that areas of Mt. Wombat were used by Aboriginal tribes for coming-of-age type rituals.

When thinking about tribes, one is guided towards thinking of origins, of family. Some cultures value ancestry more than others. In particular, Chinese rituals often include paying respects to their ancestors. The bond between disparate families is forged by way of common ancestry.

---

1 http://parkweb.vic.gov.au/explore/parks/mount-wombat-garden-range-f.f.r.

Commentary

Up until recently, the author never paid much attention to the idea of ancestors. But it is quite profound. Of course, were our ancestors not there, we would not be here. Even from a biological viewpoint, we carry the genes of our ancestors. Prior to the knowledge of genetics, people intuitively called the relationship a *bloodline*.

More than just physical traits, we carry their aspirations, parts of their nurture rather than just their nature. Even the most hardline skeptic would wish his or her future generations well — a form of prayer within itself.

The author doesn't necessarily agree with full-on rituals of ancestor worship; however, one can honour the past, and still live in the now.

If one is in a good state, respected in life, and happy, it seems that paying respects to one's ancestors seems appropriate.

Realising that our timeline travels so far back brings one to a quiet, contemplative place. One where we may draw strength from.

Wombatisms

The last section was deep. Let's talk about the wombat — the hero of our chapter — instead.

- Please do not stick your head into a wombat's burrow. Do not mess with a wombat if you know what's good for you. They pack their bodies extremely densely, and from what the author gathers, it would hurt if they hurtled themselves at you.
- Did you know the wombat has cube-shaped droppings? Fascinating stuff. The author has had afternoon walks with

7. Mount Wombat

his friends at work talking about how such a feat might be achieved. It's one of these things that you *could* look-up, but the mystery is more intriguing.

8. Shade of the Oak

Patiently the Oak grows
Deep into the Earth
High into the Heavens.

Its Inhabitants
Its Surrounds
Sustained and Protected.

Utility, Majesty, Splendour
Rising with Age.

Enchantments across Time
The Oak Absorbs
And The Oak Gives
To the Dreamers who bask
In the Shade of the Oak

Commentary

Resilience, supportiveness, and utility are defining aspects of trees. Nearly every part of many trees can be utilised towards some beneficial purpose, be it sustenance, medicinal, industrial — both traditional and contemporary, or simply aesthetic. The resilience of trees and how they support life as a whole is nothing short of a miracle.

A sight that the author is constantly in awe of is how plants manage to grow in the most barren of places, and how they break through weak points of concrete.

Adapting Utility with Age

As a tree grows, its utility adapts with this growth: bamboo shoots are edible, but grown bamboo might instead be used for furniture, or become part of a building frame.

When the tree dies, it breaks down, becoming fertiliser for newer trees. Many small growths and insect colonies live on old trees. Not all relationships are symbiotic certainly, but unless attacked by something terrible, the tree persists, letting smaller ecosystems thrive on the nutrients it provides.

This idea of age simply changing — not minimising or discarding — utility is important to understand. There is no use-by date for us if we choose to not have one. In every stage of life, one must attempt to find one's role, to contribute, and to provide value.

Making a choice to be useful also implies making choices that affect one's quality of life. To learn, so one can share one's knowledge. To be healthy, so one can perform. One cannot be of service to others without having anything to offer.

Recently, the author's friend decided to begin learning *Karaté* in his 40s — not a late age to begin by any means, but not an early age either — because he wanted to be healthier for his children's sake. That's a choice made.

On the flip side, one must attempt to see and learn of, the role of another, as objectively as is possible, rather than forcing a role to meet our perception of it, and then becoming disappointed by unmet expectations.

However, even one ailing, perhaps, due to age or otherwise, acts as a gauge of compassion in others. A role no less important.

More generally, one's utility is revealed by understanding one's role in the scheme of things. As Shakespeare wisely put it[1]:

> *All the world's a stage,*
> *And all the men and women merely players;*
> *They have their exits and their entrances,*
> *And one man in his time plays many parts,*
> *His acts being seven ages...*
>
> — **As You Like It**, Act II, Scene VII

Patience and Surrender

Many trees have lives spanning human generations. Throughout this life, the tree must withstand numerous challenges, natural and man-made. But such is its destiny to persevere through. At no point does the tree get frustrated and relinquish one or more of its roles.

Slowly (indeed, *embarrassingly slowly*), the author has gained a better understanding of patience: to persevere, but while complaining

---

1 http://bit.ly/2m9WsxA

8. Shade of the Oak

about matters, and getting bogged down by a situation, is not true patience. It is not *accepting* the situation that must be borne for the time being. Unlike the tree, in such *faux* patience, we no longer perform our roles as optimally as we can.

True surrender is a *choice* that must be made. It is not the same as giving up. To *accept* a difficult situation is to acknowledge it without blame. Neither necessarily agreeing with it, nor stopping efforts towards getting out of it, but to take a moment to clear one's mind and being.

Often, in that moment of clarity, possibilities and answers appear. No doubt this is a common phenomenon most readers will have experienced in life. Surrender, then, is followed by an action to commit to.

The author finds that the choice may need to be made more than once even within the same complex situation, for we are a forgetful kind. More so when the situation is a chronic one.

But each time made, it is powerful.

The Importance of Roots and Community

In the *Bloodlines* section of **Chapter 7 Mount Wombat**, we discussed the value of one's ancestors. Here we more holistically consider the idea of one's roots.

Ancestry, parents, community, culture, education, principles instilled — all form one's roots. They are the foundation of one's worldview. In times of difficulty, only strong, good roots hold one back from performing immoral or stupid acts.

Commentary

The author often thinks of the impact of excessive, and forced industrialisation on native tribes. Or, more generally, communities with drug and alcohol abuse problems — manifestations of weakened or lost roots.

Support groups for addictions, at their core, attempt to bring together a community. To show that one is not alone, and much more *connected*.

Recently, the author heard of the *Rat Park Experiments*[2] — concluding, in simplified terms, that rats living in a social community were less prone to morphine addiction than isolated caged rats.

Unfortunately, the experiment could not be replicated[3], "suggesting a genetic difference". The author thinks both conclusions are correct: there are certainly those who are genetically predisposed to addictions to one or more chemicals, but that a stronger community reduces the severity of addictions.

A favourite Indonesian saying[4] of the author is that only strong roots allow one to withstand the high winds.

Difficult Backgrounds

While the author is fortunate to have had a well-cared for life, there are others who may have had abusive parents or traumas of the past. This is difficult. Yet, it is inspiring to know that many people still manage to be thankful for those circumstances, for it made them better, stronger people.

---
2   https://en.wikipedia.org/wiki/Rat_Park
3   https://en.wikipedia.org/wiki/Rat_Park#Reaction_to_the_experiment
4   Likely common in other cultures, too

8. Shade of the Oak

The author has friends, and indeed, many of his masters, who grew up in bad neighbourhoods, or in difficult families. However, those who had the courage to seek a better path, to force themselves to find roots in stronger principles, first survive, then thrive.

If people with difficult backgrounds can be thankful, for those of us with a much gentler life, the need to remember our origins every now and then seems crucial.

As he writes this, the author is reminded of his Grandmaster's advice, that to forget or to deny our roots is among the gravest of sins.

To forget is already wrong. But forgetting may, in turn, lead to actions that are indeed gravely wrong.

9. Lotus in the Temple Pond

In Heat
The Lotus Blossoms.

In Murky Waters
The Lotus Thrives
In it...
But never of it.

Heart of the Pilgrim
The Lotus Draws
Towards
By its Resplendence
Inwards
By its Purity.

When Heavy, the Heart Lightens
When Light, the Heart Luminesces
At the Sight of the Lotus
In the Temple Pond.

9. Lotus in the Temple Pond

Commentary

The Lotus flower is a symbol of purity. It lives and takes root in muddy water, but remains clean. The petals remain light, carrying none of the surrounding dirt, remaining *above* it.

In the World, But Not Of It

As a teenager, when and where exactly the author can no longer remember — but a memory still strong enough to leave an impression — he met someone who first explained the symbolism of the Lotus as an analogue to humanity:

The muddy water is as the world, with all its complications — the good and the bad — where we reside.

The challenge of humanity — Lotus flowers in bloom — is to remain pure, true to their conscience, their *true nature* (to borrow a term from Buddhism, where the Lotus symbolism is possibly the most explicit) while living in the world.

We are most troubled when we don't realise that *we are not of this world*. Our true light then no longer shines through the muddiness of our situation.

The Virtues of Detachment

A certain level of detachment is also implied by the Lotus. The wisdom of detachment is implicit in everyday phrases such as 'taking the high road' and 'rising above circumstances'. Intuitively, we can already see circumstances as effectively *energies* that we can disentangle ourselves from[1].

Achieving detachment is possible by surrendering — a topic explored in **Chapter 8's** *Patience and Surrender* and worth revisiting in this context. Of primary importance is that detachment, like surrender, is not giving up or simply walking away — though, certainly, there are cases where walking away may be the correct course of action, as may be diving back in after taking stock, after taking a *breather*.

To see the bigger picture, one must detach from the everyday noise. This is far from esoteric advice, of course. We apply detachment at all levels, for example, Project Teams in Corporations have Post-Implementation Reviews, detached from the flurry of activities to see what worked, and what did not[2]. Corporations and governments also have strategic roles, distinct from operational roles, to simulate this detached view.

Transforming the Heart

The inspiration for this chapter is a Buddhist temple[3] the author occasionally visits — mostly when he has something weighing on his mind or heart.

---

[1] One of the author's favourite quote is by Nikola Tesla, the inventor to whom we owe massively scaled AC electricity: *"If you want to find the secrets of the universe, think in terms of energy, frequency and vibration.",* https://www.goodreads.com/quotes/361785-if-you-want-to-find-the-secrets-of-the-universe

[2] Though, they often miss the crucial next step — to commit to things that need to be fixed, alas.

[3] Chua Linh Son in Reservoir, VIC, Australia, see: https://www.facebook.com/pages/Chua-Linh-Son/187588484594577

9. Lotus in the Temple Pond

Sitting by the pond with a lotus flower in bloom, it's fascinating to feel the change effected, nearly in realtime.

First the heart calms down a notch. One cannot then help contemplate a situation from a detached vantage point, applying both analytical logic and feeling. One may not be able to solve the problem at hand immediately, but at least, one can walk out with a clearer view of where one stands.

Thus, one's heart is touched — *if one will let it* — then transformed, cleansed of impure emotions[4] just as the lotus transforms the muddy waters into its sublimely pure form.

---

4   The best interpretation of 'emotion' the author has heard is *Energy in Motion*.

Afterword

The hard part about writing a book of this type is that it's impossible to predict what backgrounds readers will come from. There is a danger that the author may have sounded, without any such intention, condescending or preachy. For this, he apologises.

It is also possible that the author is easily fascinated by simple things. He encourages the reader to develop the same ability.

The author takes responsibility for all imperfections in this book. All that is beautiful, all that is wise, and useful in this book, is attributed to those on whose shoulders the author stands. To those who have come before him. To the Divine Source, and, of course, to Nature, the Ancient Muse.

An errata will be maintained on the book's website at:

https://touchingnaturebook.com/

For comments, questions, or to report errors, please write to:

kamal@touchingnaturebook.com

Kindly be civil. Having only 24 hours in a day, the author cannot guarantee responses, but he will certainly make an attempt. Being civil will help, as will having a reasonably clear subject line.

About the Author

By profession, Kamal Advani has been a Software Developer for over 12 years, designing and developing enterprise systems.

His understanding of the meaning of life and living, and his drive to be closer to Nature are a result of his parents giving him the freedom to be part of the *Bandung Karate Club* (BKC) — for nearly 25 years now — where he continues to learn and teach. He bears the rank of 5th *Dan*.

This is his first book.

Colophon

Publishing has gotten a lot easier over time, thanks to technology, and the many efforts of people creating tools, often selflessly provided for free. This section documents the publication process.

Tooling

Authoring was primarily done on a **Debian Linux System**[1] using the excellent **Pandoc**[2] and its filters: **crossref**[3] and **include**[4].

Pandoc relies on LaTeX[5] and its packages to produce a printable manuscript. In particular, the author used a modified LaTeX template, and is impressed by the well-documented **KOMA - Script**[6]

Custom tooling was developed in house — quickly hacked up in **Groovy**[7] — to accommodate both EPUB — better under-

---

1 https://www.debian.org/
2 http://pandoc.org/
3 https://github.com/lierdakil/pandoc-crossref
4 https://hackage.haskell.org/package/pandoc-include
5 http://www.latex-project.org/
6 http://ctan.org/pkg/koma-script
7 http://groovy-lang.org/

Colophon

stood thanks to **Sigil**[8] — and PDF output — compressed with **Ghostscript**[9] — from the same sources, where Pandoc's native markup was lacking. **KindleGen**[10] was used to generate Amazon's **mobi** file for Kindle devices from the EPUB that Pandoc produced.

PDF sample chapters were extracted out using **pdftk**[11].

Graphics were manipulated using a combination of **ImageMagick**[12], **GIMP**[13], and **Inkscape**[14].

Finally, the build process was automated using **Gradle**[15].

Typeface

On the EPUB and Kindle formats, the typefaces have been left as defaults available on the rendering device due to annoying technical limitations. Barring Windows and Linux, it should look decent on other platforms!

The PDF Ebook and Paperback use **Mozilla's Fira Sans**[16] and the stunningly elegant **FF Reminga**[17] font family.

---

8 https://sigil-ebook.com/
9 https://ghostscript.com/
10 https://www.amazon.com/gp/feature.html?ie=UTF8&docId=1000765211
11 https://www.pdflabs.com/tools/pdftk-the-pdf-toolkit/
12 http://www.imagemagick.org/script/index.php
13 https://www.gimp.org
14 https://inkscape.org/en/
15 https://gradle.org/
16 https://mozilla.github.io/Fira/
17 https://www.fonts.com/font/fontfont/ff-reminga

Cover

The cover is a shot of the coastline at Brighton Beach[18], in Victoria, Australia. Taken on a particularly nice day while strolling with a couple of good friends.

---

18 https://en.wikipedia.org/wiki/Brighton%2C_Victoria

www.ingramcontent.com/pod-product-compliance
Lightning Source LLC
Chambersburg PA
CBHW051958290426
44110CB00015B/2293